MINDFULNESS+

Jan Janssen

INTEGRAL PRESENCE ®

ISBN 978-9-46-436430-9
NUR 770 / 728

MMXXI

Jan Janssen • www.janjanssen.be

Many thanks to Fabienne Pireyn and Mark William Britton for editorial and linguistic support and to Eva Craenhals for the graphic design.

Contents

Preamble

Meditation, mindfulness, MBSR, conscious walking, vipassana, Zen... Do you also have the feeling that you sometimes get lost in the face of the number of practices on offer today?

I'm going to disappoint you. I am bringing yet another variation with its little '**+**' sign which, though very small, comprises lots of things.

Shall we unpack it together?

1. Introduction

When I was a child, one of my favorite activities was to walk in the fields and forests near the family farm and choose a place to settle in silence. In a completely spontaneous way, this habit brought about the happiest moments of my youth. On the days when I had spare time, I would stay there for whole afternoons.

As a child I was already extremely sensitive to subtle energies. I absorbed all kinds of energetic dynamics from the human and animal worlds, in fact from all living beings. Some energetic dynamics were fine and harmonious, while others were harsh and chaotic. As a result, some days my energy field was more easily in sync with the natural world around me, but on others it was less so. Most of my time in the woods was spent harmonising with trees and animals. This apprenticeship quickly became a passion for me.

In my childhood innocence I didn't want to disturb the trees and animals with my messy vibrations, although at that age of course I didn't speak in those terms. In my vocabulary at the time I translated it as 'I will stop producing ripples in the forest'.

Practically, I liked to sit, for example, in a tree and let myself slowly slide into the calm and depth of the forest's breathing. I felt how, step by step, I could harmonise my own energy more and more with my surroundings. This harmonisation gradually enveloped me in a sweet sense of connection with trees, plants, animals and everything around me.

This is how, spontaneously, I practiced Integral Presence®, an approach which, years later, I came to dissect into its various characteristics, and to conceptualise with language: to open to others the path of rediscovering or restoring all of their human potential. This potential is often compromised or lost by non-holistic upbringings and over-adaptation to outer norms, to the detriment of inner intelligence and intuition.

At the age of 24 another overwhelming awakening experience pushed me once and for all in the direction of spiritual quest. I 'saw the Light' and from that moment, without a shadow of doubt, the conscious realisation of that Light, in myself and in the world, became my sovereign priority for the rest of my life.

What had happened to me until then without my consciously asking or wanting it became a mission for me: an irresistible path in which I had to embark consciously and voluntarily with my whole being and with the full dedication of my soul.

The years of immersing in this integral harmony gradually developed an expanded state of consciousness in my soul. The sudden shock of awakening in conjunction with this enlightened awareness created an immense tension between my soul and my mind: a mind which had been formatted by conventional education. This tension gave rise to a spiritual crisis.

I learned by reading books on psychology, spirituality, healing, religions, esotericism, the new age, cognitive science, mysticism etc.

I discovered and participated in meditation groups and workshops of all kinds, personally testing different therapies and undertaking a number of training courses. After this extensive research, I engaged in intense personal therapy, serious training in Buddhist meditation and professional training in holistic therapy.

This diversity of studies and training was very beneficial to me and helped me to achieve a knowledge and understanding of the variety of multidimensional phenomena that I had naturally experienced in my 'normal' life.
I worked diligently to synthesise my experiences and understanding into a coherent psycho-spiritual philosophy: Integral Presence® (1)

(1) "Integral Presence", Jan Janssen, 2019."

History of Mindfulness

Since the dawn of time, in many cultures and traditions, men have practised mindfulness through different means such as prayer, mantras and whirling dervishes). Meditation is an approach that is about 4000 years old.

More recently our Western culture has looked at these practices not as a fad: because they offer an infallible way to promote letting go and finding our inner peace in the face of the tumult of the world, thus leading to multiple health benefits.

In the late 1970s, various scientists discovered Mindfulness while looking at an ancient Buddhist practice. Their research into the effects of meditation on health and the brain made it possible to discover more precisely which elements of meditation, outside of cultural or religious contexts, produce mental, neurological and medical benefits.

One of these scientists is Jon Kabat Zinn, MIT Doctor of Molecular Biology, Emeritus Professor of Medicine at the University of Massachusetts School of Medicine, yoga teacher and practitioner, and meditator.
He conceptualised a specific approach called Mindfulness Based Stress Reduction (MBSR). This teaches people to use their innate resources and capacities to respond more effectively to stress, pain and illness. He thus founded the Stress Reduction Clinic in 1979.

MBSR brought together science, medicine and psychology on the one hand, with the teachings and practices of meditative traditions - known collectively as Dharma - on the other.

One of the reasons that MBSR has proven to be viable in mainstream clinical settings is that Dharma is inherently universal.

Indeed, Kabat-Zinn explains that the Buddhist origins of mindfulness reveal a phenomenological description of the nature of mind, emotion and suffering, as well as of the potential for release of mindfulness.

And 'modern' mindfulness practices are primarily focused on the systematic training and refinement of mindfulness and awareness. All these aspects like compassion and wisdom, acceptance and non-judgment, are also necessarily universal. There is nothing particularly Buddhist about them.

Mindfulness-Based Stress Reduction (MBSR) is a systematic and well-defined patient-centred educational approach based on relatively intensive awareness training. Meditation, which is at the heart of the program, teaches people how to take better care of themselves: to live a healthier and better adapted life.

This model has also been used successfully, with certain relevant modifications, in non-medical settings such as schools, prisons, athletic training and workplaces. It is an eight week program validated by thousands of scientific studies, which in turn have supported the development of a whole family of approaches that are today called '"evidence-based interventions" mindfulness for specific purposes', such as:

- MBCT - Mindfulness-Based Cognitive Therapy (Segal, Teasdale, & Williams, 2002)
- MBRP - Mindfulness-Based Relapse Prevention, for addictive behaviors (Bowan, Chawla, and Marlatt, 2011)
- MBCP - Mindfulness-Based Childbirth and Parenting (Bardacke, 2012)
- MBEAT - Mindfulness-Based Eating Awareness Training (Kristeller, Baer, and QuillianWolever, 2006)
- MBEC - Mindfulness-Based Elder Care (McBee, 2008)

The integration of these mindfulness-based approaches into medicine, healthcare, psychology, neuroscience, business, leadership, education, law and other major societal institutions is booming. We are currently seeing an explosion of interest in these practices in society as a whole.

2. Definition of Mindfulness

In 2004, Bishop and his collaborators presented a consensus document on the definition of mindfulness.

Mindfulness is:
'The self-regulation of attention so that it is maintained on the immediate experience, thus allowing a better recognition of mental paths in the present moment' and 'to adopt a particular orientation with regard to one's experience which is characterised by curiosity, openness and acceptance.'
(Bishop et al. - 2004 - p. 232)

Jon Kabat-Zinn, the pioneer of the therapeutic application of mindfulness, defines it as:
'The awareness that emerges from intentionally paying attention to the unfolding of the experience, moment to moment, and without passing judgment.'
(Kabat-Zinn, J. - 2003, p. 145)

> It is also interesting to note that in Asian languages the word 'mind' and the word 'heart' are generally translated the same. In this context, therefore, we cannot think of the word 'mind' in English without associating it with compassion with it.
> Thus, mindfulness meditative culture, whether formal or informal, involves, wherever possible, intentionally giving compassionate attention to our experience.

Yes, okay, but Mindfulness + What's that about?

I'm getting there... but I can't present the child clearly without talking about his DNA, that is to say without giving you a little feedback on the genesis of his birth, so please bear with me.

3. My journeys in Mindfulness

After my mystical experience in 1994, mentioned above, the need to understand what had happened led me, after a few months of exploring several spiritual and healing traditions, to Tibetan Buddhism.
The Vajrayana tradition, through the teachings of Tantric Buddhism, not only confirmed to me the reality of the subtle energies that I'd perceived since childhood but also provided me with a way to manage my extreme sensitivity to these energies in order to maintain the stability of my mind and psyche.

The combination of deep enthusiasm and an urgent need to embrace this receptivity has led me to train two hours a day, and sometimes more during my retreats.
My journey began with weekly meetings with different lamas (Lama Karta, Lama Zeupa, Lama Tashi Nyima) at the Tibetan Buddhist Institute in Schoten (Antwerp, Belgium) where I was advised to practice the first Shine meditation (or 'Shamata' in Sanskrit).

In 1996, I spent almost a full year at the Tibetan Institute in Huy to intensify my study and practise of the 'Shine', which gave me more stability of mind and more strength to deal with my hypersensitivity and perceptions of energetic reality. During the time of my residency there I also received numerous other Vajrayana initiations from the resident and visiting lamas, and meditation masters.

After between one and two years I was gradually exposed to more advanced practices; Shine meditation naturally leads to Lagthong (or 'Vipassana' in Sanskrit, 'Insight' in English).
Formal mindfulness practices encompass both of these practices (although this may be debated among purists / researchers, especially with regard to the Shine practice, which is more focused on concentration than attention, but our purpose here is not to open a school debate ☺).

Alongside the Vajrayana training, I got involved in energy healing practices and gave my first class in 1998.
From the year 2000, after graduating from the Brennan School in the United States, I began teaching more regularly and was asked to include mindfulness in some of my training.

Alongside the Vajrayana training, I got involved in energy healing practices and gave my first class in 1998.
From the year 2000, after graduating from the Brennan School in the United States, I began teaching more regularly and was asked to include mindfulness in some of my training.

I received permission from my teachers, Lama Karta and Lama Zeupa, to offer meditation classes, but I did not allow myself to do so until after 5,000 hours of personal meditation practice.

The studies at the Brennan School brought several complementary elements to what the Vajrayana had instilled in me, mainly in terms of psychological and relational dynamics, psycho-energetics, subtle bodies, energy healing and in the field of body-mind psychotherapy.
In addition, I trained to become a family constellation animator in 2005-2006.
Finally, the discovery of Nonviolent Communication by Marshall Rosenberg in 2008 also considerably influenced my teaching approach.

Tibetan Buddhism definition

Vajrayana :
All of Vajrayana's practices aim to achieve our 'pure being': to live in spontaneity, freedom and in enlightened awareness. They provide methods to eradicate all the obstacles that prevent touching this 'pure being' (e.g. disturbing emotions, attachments, etc.).

Specificities of Tantric Buddhism :
The specificities of the teachings of Tantric Buddhism are mainly:

- a) the maintenance of a long-term relationship between the student and his teacher in order to promote direct transmission from person / consciousness / heart to person / conscience / heart;
- b) the use of mantras, chants, visualisations, breath control, reference to archetypes of forces and
- c) recognising subtle energetic reality (e.g. chakras and energy channels) and non-physical realities (like bardos).

Shine meditation :
Sitting meditation which, in order to calm the mind, directs it to a point (i.e. proposes to focus on a specific object such as the breath and to come back to it each time the mind is left distracted).

Lagthong meditation :
A form of meditation that results in some insight into the nature of the mind.

With practice comes simplicity.

After 26 years of practising and 15 years of teaching meditation, I come to this condensed definition which, for me, covers the essence of the practice:

" Mindfulness is ...

consciously living what is."

The simplicity in the definition allows us to get to the heart of the practice. Indeed, as I mentioned above, mindfulness is a way of paying benevolent, compassionate, open and non-judgmental attention, in the present moment, to ourselves, to others and to the world around us; it is a special look and relationship to our experience which reduces unnecessary suffering and opens the way to positive personal transformation.

The result is that we live a life in which we feel and navigate the flow of life harmoniously and intelligently, allowing ourselves to be guided by its wisdom, instead of engaging in a constant and futile struggle against its immense strength.

'When you realise that nothing is missing,
the whole world is yours.'

- Lao Tze (6th or 4th century BC)

So now let's finally talk about the famous +

Little by little, the integration of all the teachings received and of my professional and personal experiences merged into a specific practice that I baptised 'Integral Presence®'. This allowed me to share the multidimensionality of life and to serve a community of students eager to know her.

My school was founded in 2012 • www.energiessubtiles.be
Integral Presence is a way to develop consciousness; it has its roots in Vajrayana, body-mind psychotherapy, family constellations, yoga practices and the Christian tradition.
Over the years, the concept has been refined and developed; it is constantly evolving, it is a living whole ☺.

Integral Presence now consists of 21 elements, the first of which is mindfulness. This is the foundation upon which all the other components can be built; it pervades them all.
A conscious presence is indeed essential to perceive all the subtle dimensions of our being (such as chakras, energy channels and many others).
If the element of mindfulness is neglected, the practise of the other components could be destabilising and overwhelming. For instance when these components are not perceived, and above all welcomed, by a benevolent neutral observation at every moment of what is. The neutral observer helps us to perceive without additions or subtractions: no judgment, no interpretation and even less rambling. Whereas, if we were to stick to mindfulness alone the other elements of Integral Presence might be accidentally discovered though we would not enjoy the same quality of understanding.

This is why mindfulness is one of the three foundations of Integral Presence, the other two being alignment and breathing. After more than 20,000 hours of meditative practice, my opinion is that it is essential that this cornerstone of several millennial traditions of contemplative art remains the basis of a contemporary practice. Indeed, thousands of years of practice by millions of yogis, monks, nuns, spiritual masters, disciples and lay people have shaped and tested its essentiality'.

Even though Integral Presence offers various complements to mindfulness, such as the other two foundations and the 18 additional elements of Integral Presence, it is always good to come back to basics no matter how far one is advanced in the complementary elements.

Without a doubt, the additional elements can increase the effectiveness of the Transformation Path and help one overcome specific obstacles. However, over-attention to additional elements can create an imbalance in practice. Therefore, it is always good to build almost every Integral Presence exercise on the three foundations and then highlight one or a few additional elements.

Mindfulness sustains all other elements of Integral Presence and together mindfulness, alignment and breathing ensure balance and cohesive integration of all elements as a whole.
Understanding of the other 20 elements of Integral Presence is not developed here. You can consult the www.integral-presence.com website or my other publications for this, such as "Integral Tranformation" and "The Art of Communion".

Thus, Integral Presence encompasses and goes well beyond mindfulness. It is a living concept that evolves with experience. As it is a work in progress, I can only advise you to 'stay tuned' ☺ -

The mindfulness that we practise in my Integral Presence trainings therefore rests both on classical mindfulness and its official exercises as explained and recognised by scientific research on contemplative practices, and also on this state of expanded consciousness in which we practise and through which initiatory currents can be transmitted to participants through intuitive channels generally little used in our western society.
This context of expanded consciousness and initiatory impact is the reason why I give it its '+' sign.

At this point, I want to invite you to do a simple little observation exercise, which I think might surprise you:

I suggest you make yourself comfortable: your back straight in a comfortable manner, your feet firmly on the ground and with your eyes closed...

Now surrender to the observation of your mind... Intend to stay in the present moment and observe...

- How does your mind relate to the present moment?
- Does it move towards the past, or does it begin to project itself in the future?
- Does a memory come to mind, or do you already think about what are you going to do tonight, tomorrow or next week... or are you suddenly thinking about what you forgot to do yesterday?

We just watch; we are not trying to force our mind into the present. We're just looking at how it behaves in terms of time. Let's observe this for five minutes...

I suggest that you take some notes on your observations about your mind's activity during this exercise, and then put them away without further thought.
I will suggest that you come back to this later...

Fancy a little discovery? https://youtu.be/QyCIJZ2QXDs

4. Key Points of Mindfulness

Attention

Attention is a key tool in practising mindfulness. Indeed, it allows one to maintain the concentration on a fixed element such as the breath, body, movement or other perceptions, and to gently bring the mind back to this element each time the concentration becomes distracted during the practice. We seek to be and stay present to what is there, in the present moment, whether pleasant or unpleasant, in all neutrality.

By developing this ability, moment by moment, we create a positive attitude towards the perpetual changes in life.
Our 'classical' or dualistic consciousness believes that what we call 'the world' is an objective reality; radical Mindfulness+ ☺, allows us to see that there are actually a lot of mental constructs in what we call 'the world'. It helps us to see with clarity that we create a whole inner world from all the information from our physical senses...
Then we give meaning to this world.

"Every negative experience becomes an invitation to reconsider the meaning we attach to events."

- Jan Janssen – September 2013

For example, two people will have a significantly different reaction at seeing the same colour depending on their appreciation, or not, of that colour. So, for the same external objective reality, different people attribute different meanings.

Usually in our fast, restless, half-conscious mind, we ignore all the intervening steps and think 'ahh red makes me happy' or 'red makes me nervous', thus thinking that the colour red has power over our experience, though this is ultimately false...

Likewise, we give positive, negative or neutral meaning to everything we perceive...
The neutral meaning already represents a next step of lucidity achieved through Mindfulness+.

Let's take a look at the steps :

- my senses pick up a colour in physical reality
- my mind builds an internal representation of the world
- I give a meaning to this inner representation
- my personal experience follows from this self-attributed meaning

We have a physical world, perception by our senses, internal representation in our imagination, attribution of a meaning, and finally constitution of an experience. There are therefore five intermediate stages between the objective world and our experience of reality!

So perhaps it's not so easy to remain in a neutral, unbiased observation of the present reality as it unfolds before our eyes, moment by moment...
Hence the need for paying reliable attention, returning systematically, as many times as necessary, and always with absolute benevolence, to this part of us whom I call the ' Neutral Observer ', a part which at all times remains exclusively in the observation of what is.

"From an honest observation, it's very striking to find
that what you are seeing is closely related
to the perspective from which you are looking."

- Jan Janssen – September 2013

Here and now

You will have understood that Mindfulness+ consists in living here and now, moment by moment, in the neutral and benevolent observation of reality.
And that's all indeed there is...

All of our experiences are phenomena happening here and now, and nothing more...
Often our minds superimpose a conception of time onto existence, so it comprises of yesterday, today and a tomorrow. But in existence there is only 'here and now'.

The past no longer exists. Try to relive, here and now, an experience from the past... it is impossible. The experience, as it was lived then, is gone forever; it no longer really exists as a concrete event, only as an interior abstraction. Everything we call 'the past' is a mental construct that is happening in our consciousness now, in this present moment.

'Oh, yesterday I saw Martine, yesterday I saw Frédéric.': it happens in the imagination
in the present moment. I tell a story... and the story that I tell is produced by me in the present moment. So, the reality of the past exists only in our present moment imagination. The past is no longer a physical reality manifesting. What is real is our present moment mental reproduction.

If I am in radical mindfulness, I can say to myself: 'ah, the suffering I am experiencing now is something that I am building in the present moment, either consciously or unconsciously. It is I who am building something in my imagination, something that makes me suffer.'

This awareness is extremely liberating for any trauma, any suffering linked to the past: it places the power over our life experience back in our own hands since it is we who are mentally constructing this suffering, detached from the present reality.

It is not our abuser, our parents, our family, or our employer who are responsible for our current suffering, but us. As long as we are under the illusion it isn't, we place the power in the hands of others: 'yes but... he said this..., and she did that..., that's what happened whereas...' and therein we lose our power.

But thanks to Mindfulness+ we know that only the present reality exists, and we learn to recognise our mental constructions for what they really are: an image we generate in our mind and not an event that is manifesting in the concrete reality in front of us.

This does not mean that we should refrain from building memories, thinking about the past, or projecting ourselves into the future. The question is not there. But Mindfulness+ develops the lucidity so, if we talk about the past, we stay aware of the fact that the whole story we tell is a construction of our mind, made in the present moment.

The events of the past are immutable. The future is shaped by the creativity of the present moment.

The events of the past have no power over us. Our experience of the present moment is determined by the significance we attach to the memories we hold about these events.
The meaning we attach to events is in our personal control. Each unpleasant experience is therefore an invitation to reconsider the meaning we attach to external events.

5. Exercise attention

We have seen that attention can help us break down the different stages that our imagination constructs to constitute our experience.
We have also seen that this awareness gives us back our power over this imaginary construct, on the way in which we live an experience, on the label, the 'colour' that we will attribute to it: happiness, misfortune, neutrality, love, hatred, emotion, serenity, etc.

You will understand that this practice requires great lucidity.
Indeed there can be, and often there is, a big gap between the reality that we construct on the basis of our sensory perceptions (smell, temperature, taste, sound, tactile and visual), which we call 'the world', and the objective reality of that same world.
The recognition of any gap between the two requires remaining in a great neutrality and in my trainings, we do this using a tool which I call the 'Neutral Observer'.
This tool is nothing more and nothing less than a partner of evolution in that it teaches us, step by step, to remain in the pure observation, without judgment, without interference, without will to change anything of what is, without ever adding any value, colour or label to the observed phenomenon.

So, we consciously live what is, **for what it is**. No more no less...

This is an invitation to live in reality, to stay in the essence of our perception instead of immediately reacting, making associations, combining this experience with past experiences and their consequences or, in short, building a whole story around present moment perception.

On the basis of even a brief experience it is clear that, generally, our mind spends a lot of time building a story. So, we spend more time imagining than perceiving...
The Neutral Observer brings us back to being in life rather than telling a story about life and immediately believing in the absoluteness of that story...

Again, I invite you to do a little exercise here and dip a toe into the water of this Neutral Observer...

I suggest that you choose an object in your environment and make it the centre of your interest for the next five or ten minutes.
As we did in the first exercise, if our attention strays from this object we return it as many times as necessary, with kindness and without judgment...

For example, I observe a blue box and I let this blue box be the blue box, I identify it as an object in the room, no more and no less...
Suddenly thoughts can arise, and I realise 'oh I'm thinking'. In this case, I just notice 'ah, I notice that I'm thinking', I recognise my thoughts as thoughts, nothing more. It is an act of discernment. Or, 'Oh I have a bodily sensation in my left knee' and when you perceive it 'I take it as a sensation, it is nothing more and nothing less than a sensation in my knee'.

Or perhaps I notice that I am telling myself a story about something my boss told me three hours ago that I'm still hooked on. I might notice I have emotions about it. In the moment I recognise 'Oh I'm telling myself a story' and 'oh I have feelings about it' I'm already at work with the Neutral Observer. I add discernment into the experience and I'm able to take a step back and realise that I perceive a story. This story is nothing more and nothing less than what I'm telling myself right now.

And I also sense my feelings about this story. And my discernment tells me, 'Oh I have a feeling... and my feelings are no more and no less than the feelings I'm feeling right now.'

This element of discernment - perceiving and consciously living what is... **for nothing more than what it is** - clears up a lot of confusion: taking our minds from the story we tell ourselves to our reality in the present moment.

I'm curious to know how you found this exercise? And I'll reassure you right away that this exercise is difficult.
Remaining in the neutrality of absolute discernment is a complex exercise for each of us. But with practice we increase the fitness of our Neutral Observer who can then develop and end up having the upper hand.

We then land into the land of the obvious, such as:
A sound is a sound.
A thought is a thought.
A sensation in the body is a sensation in the body. A mind game is a mind game.
An emotion is an emotion.
A memory that comes up again is a memory that comes up again.
A visual perception is a visual perception.
An existential question is an existential question. Hope for something is hope.
A desire for something is a desire.

Consciously living what is for what it is.

And this wonderful tool, the Neutral Observer, is always there if we ask for it. It never sleeps, never takes vacations and never goes on strike.

This is how, under hypnosis, certain people remember things that their minds have long forgotten, or that they have not consciously recorded. These people then manage to tap into what the Neutral Observer observed in reality and remember things that they did not consciously record. The Neutral Observer, loyal to the end, recorded and stored everything for them.
Our mind is always active, always subject to all kinds of fluctuations and especially so when we are having an unpleasant experience; it then wants to interfere immediately with what is being observed, while the Neutral Observer simply continues to observe what is. It has no need to change the outer reality because, by nature, it is always at peace in stillness and perfect wholeness.

Our Neutral Observer is at the heart of our consciousness. And this core is always a place of perfect peace, stillness and wholeness where there is no desire or need to change anything that is being observed.
If we befriend our Neutral Observer, we give ourselves more space to experience our reality peacefully.

Here's another little integration exercise, if you don't mind? Let's go:

I invite you to observe, for five to ten minutes, an element of your reality, of your choice, from the Neutral Observer...

And maybe you will see thoughts arise from your mind, 'Oh, this reality, I would like it more like this or like that' or 'I want more of this or less of that in my life', or 'I would like to change my relationship with so and so', etc.
And with each of these thoughts, reinvite your Neutral Observer to take action:
to be present to what is, here and now - period!

After the exercise, I suggest that you ask yourself:

- What is my tolerance for seeing things as they are, free of interference?
- Can I receive reality as it is?
- Can I extend my tolerance to allow others to be who they are, and to allow things to be what they are?
- How much do I fight against life instead of opening myself to fully receive it?

As with the first exercise, taking some notes about how your experiment unfolded can be very helpful.

By the way, talking about the first exercise... going back to your observations then, do you notice a difference in the way you performed the exercise? Is there a change in the stability of your mind during the exercise?

Exciting isn't it?

"If you want to practise more,
here is a link to meditations on the same theme."
https://janjanssen.bandcamp.com/album/mindfulness-1-4-introduction

6. What does 'being here' actually mean?

Just as it's not easy for our minds to refrain from telling stories, nor is it easy to stay 'here' and just here...

The point is to live the current 'here experience' that we find ourselves in with full awareness, and to stay present with it as it is, as it unfolds.

'Being here' means being connected to ourselves: to the state of mind we are in today, to our body as it is today and to the psychological space that we are going through. We welcome and accept it right now, just as it is.

This does not mean that the mind is forbidden to travel.
Travelling is actually one of its favourite sports ... In a millisecond we're back at the office, in a second we're already home, in a minute we're remembering our vacation on the other side of the world... So, for the mind it is so easy to travel and to travel far. Paradoxically, staying here and now is a much more challenging exercise for our wandering mind.

It is by returning to the body, to perception and to breathing that we get there.

And, again, a little observational exercise can come in handy:

For the next five minutes, I invite you to observe 'How much am I here and how much am I elsewhere?'
And don't make it a forceful exercise, because that doesn't work very well. It's not about forcing ourselves or thinking 'Oh my God I must be here, and I'm not allowed to think of anything or anybody else'. You know as well as I do that this is the best way to thinking nothing but everything else ☺.

This is just an observation exercise, it's an invitation to notice:

- Where does my mind travel to? Here? Elsewhere?
- Is it in both places? Is it coming and going?
- Where does the mind wander to?

Just be curious... be gentle with yourself...

"If you want to practise more,
here is a link to meditations on the same theme."
https://janjanssen.bandcamp.com/album/mindfulness-2-4

7. What is 'now'?

In fact, 'now' is the only time in actual existence.

Try to show me 'yesterday' or to touch 'yesterday'. Yesterday no longer exists. Try to show me 'tomorrow' or to touch 'tomorrow'. It is impossible, yesterday does not exist anymore and tomorrow does not exist yet... But our mind often makes constructions as if they both exist now.

What we call 'the past' is actually a reconstruction of what we experienced at a certain time in our imagination... but the past itself no longer exists, it is gone forever though the reconstruction that we make of it is happening now, in the present moment. After one present moment comes another, and yet another present moment, again and again: an eternal continuity of present moments.

For example, yesterday I broke my leg. The event of breaking my leg is gone. The broken leg is still there it's true, it still exists in the present, but the event of actually breaking my leg no longer exists. What remains is the reconstruction of this trauma in our current imagination.
Reliving the past is an act in the present moment. And of course, it is neither wrong nor forbidden to reconstruct the past in the present, it is even necessary, but the important thing is to be fully aware that we are doing it: to be lucid about the fact that what we call 'the past' is something that we construct in our imaginations here and now.

Likewise, it is useful and necessary to be able to make projections into the future. These projections can be reliable and perhaps close to what reality will bring, but it is important to be aware that they are not actual manifesting realities. They are a construction of our mind in the present moment, and the reality that will eventually manifest can also be very different from our projection.

The more we remain aware of this difference between expectation and reality, the more we avoid suffering and disillusionment. Any healing from trauma also occurs through this awareness of the difference between our past reality and our current reconstruction of that past. Indeed, the suffering linked to an event from the past is also a reconstruction that we make of this event in the present moment...

Until we realise this, we remain in the grip of our subconscious.
We are under the illusion that this event of the past makes us suffer today, when what really makes us suffer is the mental construction that we are making of this past event today.
This is the key awareness that gives us the power to detach ourselves from all suffering, from all trauma of the past. It is a work of radical mindfulness, of Mindfulness+.

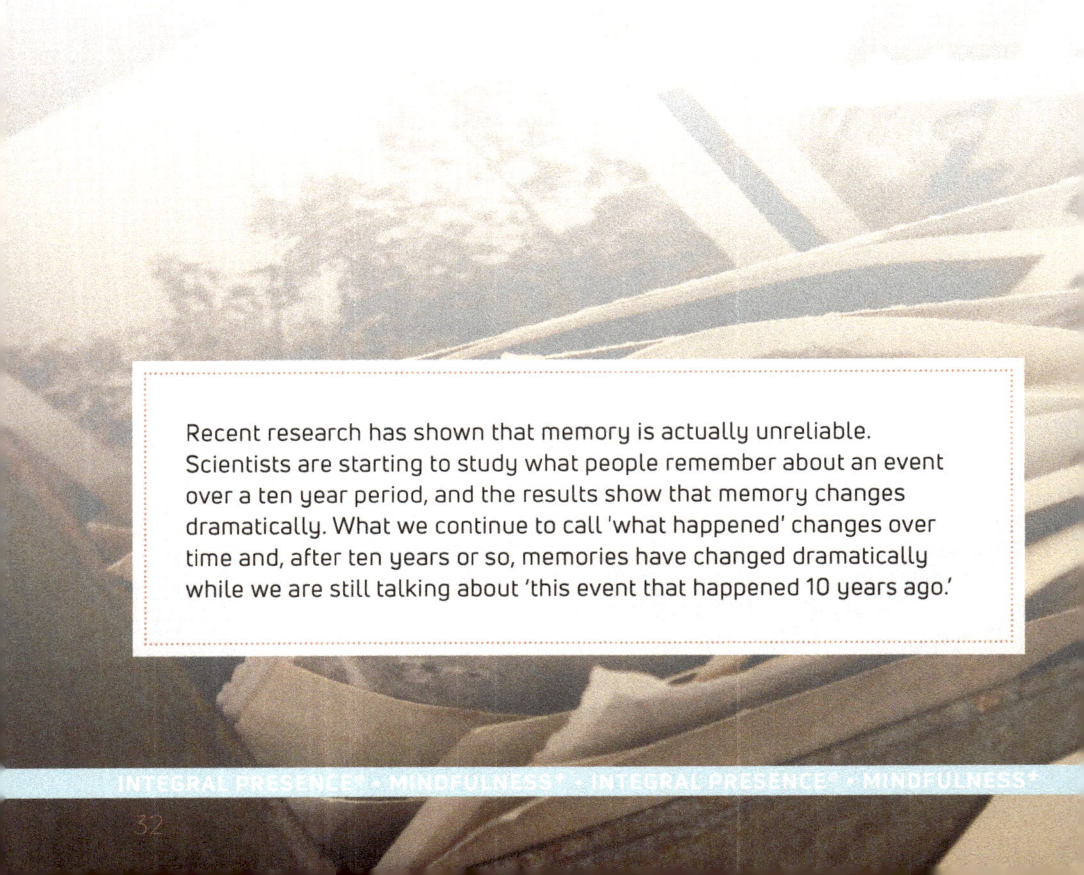

Recent research has shown that memory is actually unreliable. Scientists are starting to study what people remember about an event over a ten year period, and the results show that memory changes dramatically. What we continue to call 'what happened' changes over time and, after ten years or so, memories have changed dramatically while we are still talking about 'this event that happened 10 years ago.'

So, I invite you to visit your life experience a little.`

Let's first observe our mind for a few minutes: is my mind, my emotionality, my state of consciousness related to what is happening here in the present moment?

Or is there a memory that comes back to me, or am I already thinking about what I'm going to do tonight, tomorrow or next week... or what I forgot to do yesterday?

Do not force your mind, just observe... What does your mind do in relation to time?

Again, a little exercise of about five minutes...

"If you want to practise more,
here is a link to meditations on the same theme. "
https://janjanssen.bandcamp.com/album/mindfulness-3-4

I would like to come back to my simple definition of mindfulness :

"Living consciously what is"

... and expand a bit further on the words "what is".

My invitation is meant to build clarity.
It is obviously not a question of forbidding oneself to have memories or to plan for the future... It is very useful to plan for the future, but when we do it also helps a lot to be aware that we are planning something into the future.

This clarity allows us to identify the fears that we sometimes project into the future and to detach ourselves from unfulfilled problems that we have created in our mind in the present. So, we can find out that 'Oh, I'm telling myself a really unpleasant story about what could happen and maybe it will never happen'... What unnecessary stress and suffering!

8. The Eight Attitudes

1.
Openness
Beginner's mind, gentle curiosity

2.
Acceptance
Surrender, let go

3.
Continuity
Patience, perseverance

4.
Equanimity
Direct perception without bias, judgment, interpretation or evaluation

5.
Empathy and compassion
With detachment

6.
Gratitude
With detachment

7.
Loving kindness
Benevolent love

8.
Right effort
Neither falling asleep nor forceful focus

The eight favorable attitudes

Eight dispositions, or attitudes can be of great help to us in the practice of Mindfulness+.

And, of course, I start with my favourite: the beginner's mind.

1. *Openness*
Beginner's mind, gentle curiosity

The beginner's spirit is an openness to the actual reality of the present moment. It is a permanent gentle curiosity, as if each time we were devoid of all knowledge and discovered the world through the eyes of a child.

It is therefore very different from the expert mind. The latter always draws on all the knowledge already acquired, with a tendency to identify with it. It is therefore less available to look, with all his senses, for a possible novelty. With the beginner's mind each present moment is by definition completely new, it has never existed before. So, there can be no expertise about the present moment... Reality is produced every moment, and there are millions and millions of possibilities that the expert mind will not see because it is blinded by its identification with a future prognosis, and it conditions itself into a kind of 'tunnel reality'. The beginner's mind is an open sky, a blank page: 'wow, I know it looks like this but it's not the same thing, let's see, taste, smell... how is it right here right now?'

Take the example of our daily commute to work... it's never quite the same experience twice, we're never sitting next to the same person on the bus, it's not the same bus driver every day, there aren't the same cars around us, we do not have the same emotions, we do not have the same thoughts. Even if we think we are in a routine and everything seems the same to us on other days, nothing is less true. It is the beginner's mind that helps us glimpse these differences and savor each experience as something fresh and new: allowing us thus to really live the present reality, and not to fall asleep nor freeze us in a self-made image of reality.

The beginner's mind can have a liberating quality, but it can also confront us with our attachment, 'I have a plan for the future, and I want it to happen. I want it!'. We are then very attached to an image that we want to see come true in the future and, therefore, do not like the space that frees all possibilities.

Again, there is nothing wrong with wanting something; there is nothing wrong with having a preference and fully pursuing it.
The invitation is simply to bring awareness, clarity and freedom into this process.

"If your mind is blank,
it is always ready for anything, it is open to everything.
In the mind of the beginner there are many possibilities,
but in the mind of the expert there are few."

- Shunryu Suzuki

Do you want a taste of it? Let's...

For the next five minutes let's invite our mind to settle in the attitude of an absolute beginner and open our senses... It might immediately react, 'Yes, I already know this room, the lighting is here, the noise comes from there... I can already get an idea of this reality'.

My invitation is to stay completely blank and open to each successive present moment: every single one of them.
There will be hundreds of moments in the next five minutes.

Taste five minutes of full awareness of the present moment with the beginner's mind by waiting for another new moment, another new moment and another new moment: starting every moment from a blank sheet of awareness.

I admit that I am very curious to know a little more about your experiences. If you feel like it, do not hesitate to share your findings here: https://www.facebook.com/IntegralPresence

2. *Acceptance*
Surrender, let go

This again refers to our tendency to have strong ideas about how (our) life should be. And again, there is nothing wrong with wanting something or having a preference, but if we are very tense about it this can narrow our minds. This can then become problematic and cause a lot of suffering as we will react strongly against life, against every appearance that does not meet our expectations. This fight, besides being very tiring, always invites scarcity into our experience because life is so much richer in possibility than the imagination of a tensed mind!

Be careful, however, surrendering or letting go is not the same as becoming passive or docile. It is not submitting, or to simply want nothing anymore. That's not what it is. It's about being clear about your preferences while being open to what else life has to offer us that we may not have previously seen.

We could illustrate it with a few sentences like:

- I decide to accept this moment exactly as it is;
- I am not going to fight against what is going on right now. I don't deny it either. I welcome the present moment as it is;
- I am who I am in this present moment and I accept myself;
- My neighbours are who they are in the present moment and I accept that;
- My thoughts are exactly what they are in this present moment and I welcome them;
- My feelings and emotions are exactly what they are and I welcome them; or
- The same goes for my bodily sensations, hopes and desires.

So, I perceive reality as it is. I don't refuse to see what is, and neither do I place a barrier of wishful thinking between reality and me.

3.
Continuity
Patience, perseverance

As with any exercise, whether physical, mental, psychological or otherwise, if we hope for a result, we need to invest a minimum of commitment.
An athlete cannot hope to achieve good scores if they don't train consistently.
A researcher cannot make a discovery if they don't study at the object of their research with sufficient regularity.
And a Mindfulness+ apprentice can only achieve concentration and find alignment if they engage in regular practice...

Their effort will be returned to them a hundredfold.
moreover their life will improve as much.

However, I remind you how important it is to be gentle with yourself on this path, to remain benevolent and not to discourage yourself. I will come back to this a little later.

4.
Equanimity
Direct perception without bias, judgment, interpretation or evaluation

As I have already mentioned, with Mindfulness+, we gain lucidity and mastery over our experience of reality, that is to say over our happiness... I admit that it is no small feat ☺!

Indeed, our experience does not depend on the outside world; we are not victims of the outside world or of others with regard to our happiness or our unhappiness. This is an illusion... This also explains why two people in a similar situation can react quite differently: maybe one feels happy, the other unhappy. Has this struck you already?

Consciously or unconsciously, it is we who determine our experience; the more we become aware, the less we feel victimised, and the less we are in fact.

Because this is what it looks like when we are in Integral Presence and when our equanimity is at work:

- I feel what I feel.
- I clearly perceive my emotions, I clearly perceive my condition, I clearly perceive my feelings. I welcome them in a complete and total acceptance of what they are here and now.
- I also clearly feel my needs and accept them completely. For every need, I have creative inspiration. My imagination guides me towards the satisfaction of my needs, desires and longings. And my inspiration is not only creative but also interesting and fair.
- Then my will is awakened; I have energy, drive and enthusiasm. My will shows dynamism and flexibility; it allows me to move in the right direction according to my intuition and inspiration.
- And because I have found the right inspirations, intuitions and strategies the universe gives me results. This obviously gives me a lot of satisfaction, pleasure, fun, joy, contentment and gratitude for this cycle of creativity.
- And of course, I continue to have desires because it is a talent of our soul to generate desires. Our soul seeks to fulfill itself, to flourish. It thirsts for experiences, it thirsts for fulfillment.

And I hear you say to me, 'yes, but if we are attached to someone and we love them very much, our level of subjectivity increases and we have less of that equanimity: in the sense of being totally impartial.' And you are right. To the things and the people we love we attribute positive feelings and appreciations, and we do the opposite when it comes to things or people we dislike.

Who, in this case, can show us the way to find an absolute equanimity?

Answer :
'The Neutral Observer can.

This precious tool that I have already mentioned above.
Equanimity is a quality of the Neutral Observer.

It will always remain calm, peaceful and unchanging and will simply note, 'ah yes, of course, there my heart races because I love that person or there I rebel because I condemn such activity'. It will remain in total lucidity, in the discernment of what is happening in us, and our equanimity will therefore not be disturbed on that level of perception.

5.
Empathy and compassion
With detachment

Empathy and compassion are two basic attitudes that can make our experience more harmonious and make us suffer less from fluctuations in the course of life.

If we are faced with a painful event, for example, we can be overwhelmed by the hardness and difficulty in which we find ourselves and thus find it difficult to move forward calmly. Or we can resort to all kinds of strategies such as denying, minimising, projecting onto others etc. In this way we don't feel the emotions linked to this event.

If, on the other hand, we create a space of love, compassion and empathy in our heart then we can embrace the difficult experience, emotion or feeling. We can dare to feel it fully instead of fighting it: we can integrate it.

Thanks to the Neutral Observer we can also observe what old memory this experience revives, what trauma it resonates with. Utilising the observant neutrality and detachment of the Neutral Observer we clearly perceive what is happening without going into any form of dramatisation.

And let me add that 'detachment' does not mean indifference... Indifference is a wall that we build between ourself and our experience so as not to feel. While with detachment we are fully in the experience but we don't hang on to it, we are not adding drama in the present moment to the past experience.
As soon as we are clear about our suffering we either automatically heal it, or we have the choice and the power to change it into happiness.

6.

Gratitude

With detachment

In the face of pleasant experiences too, we can react in two different ways:

- Either we cling to it, 'Oh, I want to live that again, I want to keep this feeling...'. This clinging induces a sort of 'cramp' in the mind and turns out to be very counterproductive since we are no longer open to all of the potential new 'fresh' experiences;
- Or by refusing the pleasurable experience, the pleasure, for fear of suffering when the experience is over, which is just as counterproductive.

That's why, I want to talk to you about detached gratitude: fully living the pleasant experience with grateful detachment. This says 'I know it's there now. I'll take full advantage of it and as long as it is there. But I also know that it will turn into something different. And I feel good with that too. My energy flow is going to change all the time because life is always changing.'

And besides it's the same with pain, 'Ok, this is what I am going through now, I will embrace this with all my love and my compassion. I also know that it will change because life is uninterrupted movement.'

7. Loving kindness
Benevolent love

When trauma resurfaces, as we have seen before, our task is to bring clarity to our current experience of this trauma.
This lucidity can only happen if we are kind to ourselves and when we have a lot of empathy; trauma can be very painful. It is a human need that the pain and emotions that go with trauma are not only fully seen but also welcomed into a bath of kindness, empathy and compassion. They can then subside and our story, which is in this case truly recognised and understood, can let go of its insistence. From then on, our trauma somehow becomes more malleable to change. And we can move forward on our way...

When I speak of 'loving kindness' to yourself or to others, it is therefore not a romantic feeling, it is a benevolent love which has the capacity to make us find the lost balance. It is some kind of homeostasis of the mind. After we have been able to burn all the fears, all the anxieties, all the faults of the functioning of our little 'I', by putting them in the loving light of benevolence, there remains only pure beauty and goodness. It will become obvious because beyond the little I, there awaits us a perfectly balanced, pure and good being, able to act with confidence, courage and love, who moves from one act to another with ease and who says what is right at each present moment.

And by the way, I'll give you a little 'trick', and that is that practising this loving kindness works great if we apply it to our physical bodies too. When we treat our bodies with loving kindness - not in complacency, nor in rejection - but in a benevolent lucidity, we get on our own side and give ourselves the chance for our body, as well, to find a perfect state of homeostasis and therefore best possible health.

8. Right effort

Neither falling asleep nor forceful focus

The principle of right effort is also very important. To illustrate this I can compare it to walking. If we walk without any drive, we are dragging ourselves forward and walking will not be of much benefit; on the other hand, if we put too much force into it, we will very quickly exhaust ourselves and maybe even strain a muscle. The right amount of effort will allow body and mind to benefit from an invigorating walk, without excessive fatigue.

The right balance in effort is also a form of homeostasis.
It is the same in meditation, in Mindfulness+:
If we don't pay attention, we will daydream and maybe even fall asleep;
If we exert too much attention effort, all of our concentration goes to mental effort and we lose the object of focus.

In balanced vigilance, all of our focus goes to what is present, here and now.

A little exercise to close this chapter?

Let us decide to get to know our rib cage, applying the principle of 'just effort'...

We can choose to start paying attention to the diaphragm and, with this attention, without being in the forcing of 'wanting to feel', we can simply let ourselves 'slide' into the perception and feel that it contracts when we inhale and or relaxes when we exhale. It therefore begins to exist in our experience of reality. Let's stay present to these movements for a few moments...
We can then focus on our rib cage itself; all the ribs that unfurl under the influence of inhalation and return to their retracted position under the influence of exhalation... And now our ribs and our intercostal muscles have also acquired an identity in our experience...

This allows us to 'bring to life' any part of our body as we choose.
And you will observe that in each of us certain parts of the body are easier to get to know than others. This is normal and I invite you to observe this without judging, without any performance mentality, just with loving kindness...

Here too, it can be useful, on your path of progression, to take some notes about your observations, or even to illustrate your observations with a few sketches: which parts of the body are revealed very easily, which other parts tend to remain more 'silent'?
And I invite you to compare your observations over time... I'm sure you will be surprised at the result ☺.

With practice, we live more and more fully in the present moment and these eight attitudes occur more easily and spontaneously.

Below are the references to four guided meditation albums and explanations that can help you build or deepen your Mindfulness+ practice.

▶ https://janjanssen.bandcamp.com/

9. What is Mindfulness+ not?

To better understand what Mindfulness+ is, it can be useful to examine what it is not.

All mindfulness practices involve some form of meditation. However, in the West, misconceptions about meditation are legion. Let's take a look at some of the most common misconceptions below.

A. It's not about clearing your mind

If we go back to our definition of Mindfulness+: 'consciously living what is (here and now)', it is therefore a matter of perceiving our current experience through the gaze of the Neutral Observer. A good starting exercise can be to look at the contents of our mind, to look at our thoughts. When a thought arises, we don't repress it, we realise 'ah, I perceive a thought' without being carried away by it in a mental progression.

So, it is not about preventing the mind from having thoughts, but rather training the mind to be aware of what it is doing at all times. Preventing thoughts doesn't work as the mind is made to produce thoughts, and it will continue to do so even if we are meditating.

Thus, we learn to be aware of the existence of our thoughts, without wanting to 'do' anything with them: not fighting them, suppressing them or taking reactive action based on them.
It's in this way that we learn to detach ourselves from our identification with thoughts and simply observe what our usual thought patterns are.

It may be that our mind is blank when we are in mindfulness, but this is a side effect of meditation and not a goal. The goal is the pure and simple observation of our thoughts and the functioning of our mind.

B. It's not about getting over emotions

Some people seem to hope that the practice of Mindfulness+ will relieve them of the burden of emotions, especially for difficult emotions such as distress, grief, jealousy etc.
However, in reality, Mindfulness+ practice often has the opposite effect in the beginning: as we train ourselves to observe the contents of the mind, we come to notice our emotions more fully and vividly. Our ability to recognise what we are feeling increases as we let go of our usual defences to simply observe what is happening within us here and now, without barriers.

In general, when emotions become more intense, we may find it difficult to maintain our lucidity. It is again the development of the Neutral Observer within us that will allow us to recognise the emotion we are experiencing and to feel its intensity, is it: concern, apprehension, fear, anguish or perhaps terror? The non-judgmental reception of all our emotions, whatever they may be, facilitates the emergence of lucidity. If we start to judge ourselves or to fight against our emotions then our energy is lost in unnecessary twists and turns. It is the unconditional reception of all our emotions in all their breadth, intensity, and depth that ensures our pursuit in clarity and creates security for the deeper work of the soul.

When we encounter suffering it is always linked to the fact that we do not accept 'what is' for what it is, on the contrary we add negative interpretations to it. I think 'ah today, they don't not want to see me...', and if I accept it as it is, I do not suffer. If, on the other hand, I add an interpretation such as 'they don't want to see me therefore they don't love/like me any longer' then I suffer.

Being able to free ourselves from suffering involves healing our wounds because they are what prevents us from genuinely welcoming life as it is now.

To train us a bit in this ability of remaining lucid in the presence of our emotions, I suggest that you revisit the most recent event in which you felt strong emotions.

And then to make a commitment to yourself: 'I'll stay clear and revisit this episode. I'll look with clarity at the stimulus that provoked this emotion'. And I'll also perhaps observe my first reaction: did I fight against it, did I repress it or deny it?

Next, let's observe the emotion itself with direct perception: what is its colour, taste, smell, feeling, intensity, magnitude, duration etc always without any judgment. Finally, at what point did the emotion dissolve, subside or transform into another emotion?

This self-help with lucidity helps us to release and transcend the emotions.

C. It's not about being calm or being different

While it is true that a feeling of peace, calm or relaxation can be experienced while practicing mindfulness these are not guaranteed results. Mindfulness+ is simply noticing any present moment experience that we go through including any thoughts, feelings or physical sensations that are part of it, be them pleasant, unpleasant or neutral.

Going through all our experiences in the simple observation of what they are, without adding artificial constructions to them, and remaining in the calm of our natural strength, in the centre of our body, in the dantian, allow us to be strong by nature and not by willful force, which is much more powerful and effective.

Some people think of mindfulness as trying to become unabashedly calm. That's not what it's about. This can be a side effect and, if you practise regularly, it is likely that some sort of basic serenity will settle into your consciousness. But it is not something that we can produce voluntarily, it is something that will arise spontaneously over time with regular practise. We cannot force ourselves to be serene by repeating to ourselves, 'I will be serene... I will be serene', that does not work; on the contrary, we then create a lot of tension.

The only way is to keep paying attention, over and over again... It then comes gradually and naturally, not by force.

The dantian

In Eastern traditions dantian, also called 'ocean of energy', is considered the centre of instinctive and intuitive life on which all our physiological and psychological functions depend.

It corresponds physiologically to the centre of gravity of the human body. Dantian is important for meditation, and for practicing qigong and Chinese martial arts, but it is also and above all our centre of natural strength, as opposed to our voluntary strength.

As we focus our attention on our dantian, we immediately observe a feeling of vitality accompanied by great calm.
If we fully focus on the present moment, the energy of dantian increases.

"Most of our ailments are caused by the loss of contact with our 'hara'"

- Jacques Castermane, Director of the Dürckheim Center

D. It's not about reducing stress

It's not about reducing stress, even though Mindfulness+ can effect this considerably!

Mindfulness+ teaches us to manage our concerns differently, to react to stressful experiences in a healthy and adapted way.
Stress is the result of an accumulation of undigested life situations. By helping us to explore in a neutral way how we relate to stressful events, and what links we develop with these events, Mindfulness+ opens our lucidity. With the glasses of the Neutral Observer a fine integration of these experiences becomes possible, which will reduce stress levels in a natural way ensuring they don't build.

E. It's not about escaping pain

Rather than attempting to escape pain Mindfulness+ practice helps us increase our capacity to endure it, welcoming it into neutral observation and deliberately refraining from automatic actions designed to make us to feel better.
For example, if we are meditating and an itch occurs a typical instruction is to observe and feel it, noticing any impulses that arise (like the urge to scratch for example), but not to react immediately to it.

Therefore, we feel pain or discomfort more vividly. And it can go beyond itching or physical pain to include the whole spectrum of emotional ailments as well.
When we accept the exploration of these unpleasant experiences with lucidity and neutrality our capacity to endure them increases.
We also discover that painful sensations (physical or emotional) are distinct from the suffering that accompanies them. We find that suffering occurs when we respond to pain with resistance, protest or avoidance rather than momentary acceptance.
Mindfulness+ thus helps us to not flee our experience of reality and opens us to the depth of our higher consciousness which resides beyond all pain and suffering.

If we see suffering as a signal of dualistic perception of reality, and use pain as a motor to process and transform the root cause of this suffering we are on the road to recovery.

The next step will then be the curative confrontation: meeting the trauma with the reality of the present moment. The realisation comes when the incident that caused the trauma is a thing of the past, that it is no longer necessary to 'carry' it, which is always a moment of liberation, 'Ah yes... I see that the incident that happened in the past no longer exists here and now. I clearly perceive the impression that it left and I perceive the reality of the present moment as clearly.'

Three different things then: the reality of the present moment, the feeling that I still have in my soul about this incident from the past, and the incident from the past itself. They are three different things. And once one has reached that degree of lucidity and discernment between the incident, its impression and the reality of the present moment, one can let go of the trauma. One can choose to maintain the impression, to let it go altogether, or to let go of the emotional charge around it. The latter means that memory of the event can be retained, but one can let go of the negative charge attached to it.

Suffering, therefore, comes from what we do with the unpleasant experience, but the experience itself does not have the power to make us suffer.
From then on, complete healing of the trauma can take place: we have the memory of the incident, the memory of the impression it created and the memory that we have suffered a lot. We also choose to let go of the suffering and come back to the current reality in our pure consciousness.

We thus acquire a wisdom of life and knowledge about the creation of suffering and how to get out of this suffering. The bumper sticker I saw on the car of a Buddhist monk summarised this perfectly,

'Life is painful, suffering is optional'

F. It's not about complacency

Acceptance does not mean agreement, complacency or resignation. It means recognising what is happening… because it is already happening anyway… We are then able to make decisions and take actions to change a situation when it is appropriate for our well-being and that of others, but we do it out of compassion and understanding, instead of doing it from opposition or impotent frustration. Mindfulness+ teaches us to be radically honest with the reality of life.

It invites us in particular to detach ourselves from wishful thinking and replaces it with a clear vision. It encourages us to intentionally dismantle our idealised images of self, others and life so that the pure truth of self, others and life can appear in our consciousness.

In my trainings, we call this work 'the Cycle of Transformation'. Much like Mindfulness+ the cycle of transformation emerges from true inner compassion and positive creativity not from a place of defence, which makes all the difference when it comes to the results it generates.

G. This is not a technique

Mindfulness+ is not a technique. Rather, it is about learning a new way of dealing with the things that trouble us instead of trying to make them go away.
By practicing mindfulness more and more, our Neutral Observer acquires more space in our mind and we then live more consciously, precisely and more in adequacy with the events.
Mindfulness+ thus goes beyond being a practice and becomes a way, or quality of being.

H. This is not a miracle pill

Mindfulness+ is not a magic pill. A Mindfulness+ session is not an object of consumption to solve a problem. When we are stressed or going through a difficult time we habitually look for 'techniques' to help us cope better.
And Mindfulness+ can help us as long as we approach it with the right scope: that of a long-term vision. It could be called 'slow medicine for stress'.

The repetitive practice and thus development of the Neutral Observer tool, which we have already spoken about several times, allows us to nurture an inherent link with the natural peace that exists at the centre of our consciousness. This peace is present no matter what fluctuations of life may come our way.
This indestructible inner peace is always there, accessible at every present moment.

I. This is not a religious practice

Despite having its roots in the Buddha's era, mindfulness is not about religion (and Buddhism is not a religion by the way). It evolved and became the fusion of millennia of Eastern philosophy and the latest findings in Western psychology. That's what makes it so beautiful.

However, all religions could benefit greatly from any kind of mindfulness practice. It is truly useful to everyone whatever their spirituality, religion, background or beliefs. It is a human experience that calls for the development of awareness and compassion: things that are found in all of us.

The Integral Presence does not offer any belief system. It invites each of us to question our personal belief system in the light of a new lucidity and to find one's truth in every present moment.

J. It's not about retiring from life

Because most meditation practices were originally refined by monks, nuns and hermits, people often think of it as a choice to withdraw from life. Nothing is less true.

Even if one practises mindfulness in a simplified, austere or withdrawn environment, one does not withdraw from life. On the contrary, the vicissitudes of life are lived more vividly because we take the time to focus our full attention on our experience of the present moment and to live it fully, with all that that entails. We are therefore fully in life and work more consciously for life.

Mindfulness is not about seeking happiness either, but it is often a side effect.

K. It's not about seeking bliss

The image of the spiritual master smiling blissfully while the rest of us struggle with existential reality is very startling but misleading. At the start of their meditation career, many people judge themselves when they find that their mind is wandering, and they are restless or confused. It can be helpful to know that all of these conditions are very common and will inevitably recur.

Our soul also often works with a whole series of images: one image comes after another and another, then yet another. And just like in the cinema, when one image comes after another a film is made. Our soul often takes care of producing inner movies: telling apparently very real stories including characters, plots and an ending... It is a normal activity that gives meaning to our life because physical life by itself has no inherent meaning; it is our soul that gives meaning to all of our experiences.

And here too, bringing lucidity into the mechanism of 'the inner movie maker' to realise that it is an activity that belongs to us, and not one imposed by an external movie director. Even understanding that we can choose not to undergo this passively is a huge learning. From that moment on we are no longer a victim of life. We become the author of our life.
Therefore, at the level of our spiritual path it is evident that it helps to move us towards enlightenment.

10. How to practice Mindfulness+?

A. Level 1 body scan: fill the body with attention

One of the basic techniques for practising Mindfulness+ is simply to focus attention on the body: scanning each part of the body in turn, centimeter by centimeter, and feeling what is being experienced from instant to instant. We stop at each part of the body: bones, skin, organs, digestion etc. This is an effective method for developing concentration and flexibility of attention simultaneously.

I suggest you start your personal scanner.

Place your body in a comfortable seat, preferably with your feet on the ground: to promote the circulation of energy.

We start with the feet, turning our attention to the soles of our feet: the sole of the left foot first and then the sole of the right foot.

Then we progressively pay attention to the:

- toes of the left foot
- toes of the right foot
- both feet
- left ankle
- right ankle
- calves on both sides
- shins: the bones of the lower leg
- knee joints
- the femurs: the thigh bones
- thighs
- pelvis
- pelvic floor
- hips
- lower abdomen and its contents
- higher abdomen and the contents of the abdomen

- spine
- all the vertebrae
- diaphragm
- chest
- ribs
- chest contents
- lungs
- heart
- shoulders
- arms
- forearms and elbows
- wrists, hands and fingers
- throat and neck
- head
- face
- skull
- mouth
- tongue
- nose
- eyes
- ears.

And finally, the focus is placed on the whole body.

As you can see, it is really about patiently and deliberately 'dissecting' our bodily sensations area by area and step by step. It may seem a bit tedious at first glance, but I urge you to give it a try. You will quickly see the kind of calm it settles in you.

B. Mastery of the mind level 1: staying in the 'now'

Another interesting approach is that of observing our mind in relation to time.

In the practice proposed below, I invite you to take an interest in the present moment...

The present moment is unique at every moment. 'This is obvious!' you will say to me.
I'm not sure it's really obvious to all of us every moment. Let's take a look at this question a bit:
The present moment, even when we conjure up a memory, is never an event from the past that would appear a second time. It is not like a movie that we could rewind to watch the exact same images a second time.
Nor is there ever an event from the future that we could summon with the mind to make it arise in the present here and now reality.

Our whole life is therefore only a succession of unique present moments. The moments of the past no longer exist: when I recall them, it is a mental production that I've created in the present moment that exists.
The same goes for the future: it doesn't exist yet. Of course it is necessary to think about the future sometimes, to plan things, but that too is a mental production that we do in the present moment; things might turn out to be different than we expected when we actually arrive at this future time. The actual circumstances that manifest may well reveal many completely unforeseeable things.

Therefore, we cannot experience life except in the present moment.

The characteristics of the present moment are therefore singularity, uniqueness, originality and non-reproducibility.
Admit that this makes it a magical moment!

Let's stay a little while in silence with this new awareness of the present moment...

C. Body scan level 2: fill the body with consciousness

Let's now take the experience one step further. We previously filled the body with attention; we now fill it with consciousness. How? 'Or' What?

This time, we don't just bring our attention to the different parts of the body, we proceed to a direct perception of our body: we 'let in' the perceptions and receive the sensations instead of shifting our attention to different parts of the body.

We can take the example first of the feet and the direct perception of sensations in the foot: the pressure of the shoes, the pressure on the ground, the texture of the socks etc.
Then the direct perception in the calves: the force of gravity exerted on them, the texture of our pants, the muscles which may be relaxed or on the contrary a little tense. Then, direct perception of our knees and in the knees: the placement of our kneecaps, the angle in which our leg is bent... Now bring direct perception to our weight on the chair, the back pressure of the chair against our skin, the muscles below the gluteal bones which are compressed and the muscles around them which are less compressed.

As you can see, we can extend this reception of sensations to the whole body. This approach is much more lucid than a general body scan. This is the most direct step to be in the present moment, completely, directly.

> At the same time as we focus our attention on the different parts of the body, we allow silence to enter the body: we perceive it as a substance that enters each of our cells and has an effect on each of them. Let's observe...
>
> With a broader quality of attention, we let the silence mix with the breath; we not only take air into the lungs, but we also let that silence enter the lungs.
>
> This silence is not limited by physical constraints like air, which is limited to the space of the lungs. The silence can penetrate and extend everywhere in the body.

In opening up our whole body to it we can discover very simple things, 'Oh! I have never felt each of my toes as I do now', which moreover is strictly true as my feeling at the moment has never existed in a similar way before and will also be different from how I will feel them later.

I can also play with this expanded awareness and, for example, carry a little more awareness in my right knee than in my left knee, and then bring equal awareness to both sides. Consciousness is an extraordinary tool, it significantly changes my experience, the way I live my body...

Finally, I suggest you take a quick look at which part of your body is more conscious today, and which is less? Just as information, there's no call for anything performance related...

It is normal that some parts of our body are more directly 'accessible' to consciousness and others less. It is the same for everyone. I invite you to simply observe this state of affairs without judgment, and with the trust that through repetition the body will become more and more receptive for consciousness.

D. Mastery of mind level 2: stay here and perceive

This time it is another form of training the consciousness: the observation of thoughts.

Let us sit down and invite our Neutral Observer to accompany us...

The nature of our open mind is like a great sky, in which clouds of thoughts pass. I observe that a thought arises and takes up space in the sky of the open mind. Perhaps it turns into another thought or takes a trip. Then the cloud of thought changes shape, 'Oh, a thought started like this and suddenly it becomes like this and then like that. I started with this one thought and now here I am with this other thought.'

What malleability!

Simple observation, just with loving kindness...

We don't cling to any of these thoughts. We just let the Neutral Observer watch them play out: generation, movement, modification and dissipation. We do not enter into debate with any of our thoughts; we simply stay present and perceive, no more and no less...

E. Body scan level 3:
fill the body with presence

After the first two steps of the body scan technique:

1. Bringing our attention to all parts of the body; and
2. Receiving more bodily sensations and qualities of perceptions in our consciousness,

...we move on to the next step...

3. Filling the body with presence.

So, now we are working with three elements: attention, awareness and presence.

Let's turn our attention to our skull this time...

Do we have a perception in our skull? Do we feel our hair on top of our head? Do we feel the temperature of our skull? Do we feel our brain in our skull? How much consciousness do we have of our skull?
And with this awareness, I invite you to bring a presence: an unconditional presence. This brings an element of wholeness in addition to awareness.

Then apply these same qualities of attention, awareness and presence to our face, forehead, eyes and eyelids. What do we perceive in our eyes with attention, awareness and presence? Are they relaxed, moving, tense, open or closed? Do we have visual perception or not?
No matter what reality is there we take it as it is, and bring to it neutral attention, open awareness and gentle presence.

We bring attention, consciousness and presence to each part of the body that we choose to explore...

We all now know the powers of the mind over the body; the placebo effect is one of the most recognised phenomenon in medical science. We could very well call Mindfulness+ a 'positive and deliberate use of the placebo' because it has a positive effect on our body through the deliberate use of our mind.

The intention of the practice of Integral Presence is to make the most of this positive power of the mind: to train the mind in consciousness and emancipate its full potential.
The regularity of this practice allows us to refine our sensitivity to the body's signals. The body constantly sends us information on its proper functioning, its state of health and its needs. Are we paying enough attention to it? Let us offer it this benevolence daily; let us embody ourselves fully!`

F. Mastery of the mind Level 3: observation of feelings and sensations

This practice is particularly useful in learning how our physical experience relates to our emotional experience and vice versa.
Each emotion that crosses us has its particular way and its favourite place to reside in the body.

By opening our attention to receiving this information, we can begin to learn how to better respond to physical and emotional signals.

To feel and to perceive sensations, feelings and emotions... To observe... It can be very useful to then find one, two or three words to describe and confirm' our experience.

> Let's focus on our feelings and emotions using the example 'I'm angry'...
> Instead of jumping into immediate reactivity, let our body give way to this anger, let it circulate in the body...
>
> This allows us to 'hold our horses' a bit and to have a little space to think, 'ok, the emotion is here but what is the best action here and now?', while simply allowing the emotion to exist.

Sometimes someone says, 'yes but at the moment I have no feeling or emotion'; this is impossible unless you are physically dead. Every living creature, at every present moment, has a quality of feeling, of emotion, in it otherwise we just aren't alive.
It may be that our feeling is calm, tranquil or peaceful and therefore attracts less attention; this does not mean that it does not exist!

Be consciously experiencing what is happening at the feeling level right now: here and now... What is real to me in this present moment at the feeling level?

Very often, there is a cocktail of feelings...

> What's in my cocktail right now?
> Does it have a taste of peace, a texture of anxiety, a flavour of joy, a spark of curiosity, a hint of anger, a volcano of rage or perhaps an ocean of sadness? It is even possible that there are paradoxical emotions in this present moment: love and hate at the same time, attraction and repulsion at the same time, excitement and fear at the same time...
>
> What is my cocktail of feelings in this present moment?

There are six basic emotions that run through our system: fear, anger, sadness, disgust, surprise and pleasure. These are the six primary emotions. Then there are a lot of social emotions like attraction, repulsion, love, friendship, guilt, shame, pride etc.

How do we feel in the midst of others, of a group? It's a safe bet that still more feelings or emotions will emerge like contentment, frustration, anxiety, courage, excitement, boredom, enthusiasm, discouragement, melancholy, bubbling joy etc.

Let's get into the habit of doing a little check in of our emotional and feeling state during the day.

"Nervousness is excitement in the making"

- Jan Janssen – September 2013

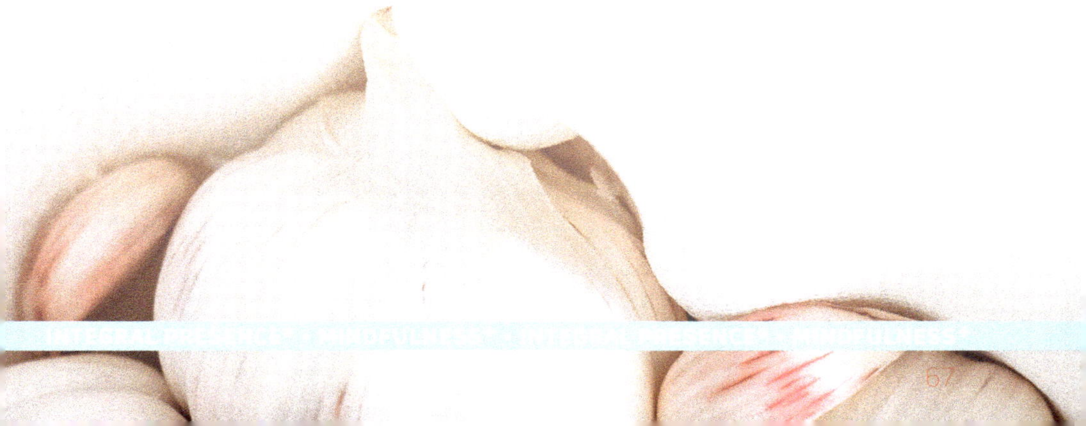

G. Body scan level 4: fill the body with loving kindness / light

Some days when we fill our body with presence, the depth of our practice is greater and all of a sudden we have the happiness of seeing a kind of grace emerging from the depths of consciousness.

This grace is a kind of energy which penetrates and envelops us at the same time, and which has a great influence on our body. It purifies and it builds all at the same time.
It purifies darkness, ignorance, unconsciousness, egoism, rigidity, fear, negativity and blockages.
And it builds: bringing light into every cell, into every atom of our body, into every corner of our soul.

It deifies the physical body and the soul; it is a descent into the supra-mental lights. To benefit from it, we have nothing else to do than welcome and surrender to it...

A little try perhaps? Let's...

Let's start with the attention as we have already done; with a little practise, our attention becomes more refined, deeper and more real.

How does my foot feel right now? Suddenly our consciousness is in greater relation to our foot so an intimate conscious connection with this part of the body can take place. And this intimate connection is a wonderful basis for going even further: bringing presence; this is yet another quality. Our foot carries us every day, it allows us to move, jump and dance. Then let's bring loving kindness to it, 'thank you my feet, for your good and loyal service'.

We can of course do the same for all parts of the body and all of our organs. They do a brilliant job, 24/7, of maintaining homeostasis in our system; they deserve some gratitude...

Giving some kind attention to the diaphragm is also a good exercise. In modern society our body tends to store a lot of stress in the diaphragm so it is good to pay a little more attention to this part: freeing the stress and tension by bringing presence and loving kindness into it. By releasing the stress from the diaphragm the breath opens up and we suddenly breathe more freely. And every movement up and down of the diaphragm is also a gentle massage of the lungs and abdominal organs. It is a little caress each time. Thus, our diaphragm, with each breath, is also our internal massager .

'Do I sense my breathing? Do I sense my heartbeat? Do I hear my heartbeat?' Bring presence and loving kindness to the chest. Bring loving presence to the chest with its heart and lungs.

And to my arms and hands which are also wonderful instruments! I use them daily, so many times, for so many things. Imagine you are missing a thumb: it would be so inconvenient. This is just one example of the amazing instruments our arms and hands are. They deserve loving kindness, appreciation and gratitude.

And what about my brain sending its signals to my muscles to move and orient in the right direction? There's no need to think about it... If we want to have a drink, we just have to think about doing that. However, to actually do it in one smooth movement the brain has to send many signals to many muscles in perfect coordination and timing, and also with the right effort: not too much, not too little.

It's an intelligent, astonishing, clever and complex system! And it is so easy for us to use this complex system. So, the brain also deserves a lot of attention and gratitude, as does the skull for protecting our brain.

We can also thank our body for maintaining cerebrospinal and brain fluids in perfect balance, rhythm and pressure: if there was too much pressure, we would have a headache all day, and if there wasn't enough pressure, our brain would be damaged.

Let's not hesitate to thank our body for this permanent work of homeostasis; let's show it gratitude and kindness...

H. Level 4 mind control: continued concentration, through breathing

Nature has given us a fabulous tool: breathing!
This is of course used to meet the oxygen needs of our body, but not only that... We can also use it to stabilise our mind and thus increase our ability to concentrate.

Let's take a closer look...

As always, I suggest that you make yourself comfortable for the meditation that follows; you now know the importance of good posture.
When you are settled, I invite you to observe your breathing... Just observe for now, without wanting to change anything. Focus on the inhalation... and then on the exhalation. Do this for several full breaths.

Then, focus on the inhalation making sure you stay there for the duration, from the first second to the last...
Now do the same thing for the exhalation...

Then observe the momentary pause that separates the inhalation from the exhalation... Oh, it doesn't last long... But spot him and stay 'with' him in full awareness for that little while.

Finally, assemble the observation of all these moments and keep your attention on your breath throughout the entire process: inhale pause, exhale, pause / inhale, pause, exhale, pause etc.

Can you feel the calm that this instills in you?

Smilefulness

SMILE

As said above, for me there is a great relationship and a real power of the mind over the body. This is demonstrated every day by the placebo effect which, I believe, is unfortunately not sufficiently exploited for the benefit or our health. This is why I am so eager to teach the practice of mindfulness and Integral Presence: this quality of potential positive influence of the mind over the body. I think that's worth cultivating and maximising.

Five years ago, I discovered that when I am happy, homeostatic and in good shape, smiling happens naturally. And so it is for many people; when all is well, a smile comes naturally to us. Smiling is actually the outward expression of inner homeostasis and well-being.

I have also noticed that a smile from another person has a wonderful effect on me. If someone smiles at me, it feels so very nice. It immediately has a positive mental effect and my body relaxes.

So, I decided to start practising smiling during mindfulness by making sure that it is found everywhere in my body; it has a delicious effect!

An invitation for a trip to the land of smiles...

Sit in a comfortable seat for your body and, by applying the right effort, let the be: observe it without wanting to transform it... Pay attention to your heart: it beats like this every day, but, today, decide to allow it to beat with a smile. Feel that smile in your heart; it is there.

And notice the lungs breathing, like every day, twenty four hours a day, but now let's breathe a smile into the lungs.

And there's the liver that produces all its chemicals and balances so much in our digestive and circulatory systems. The liver will continue to do so, but this time with a smile.
And there's also the stomach, maybe it's a little hungry, maybe it's full, maybe you have just eaten, but right now the stomach decides to digest with a smile. It smiles at the food that is already there, or that is coming...

There's the pancreas too, which manages the level of glucose in our blood... it does it every day but right now the pancreas is smiling.

And the spine smiles, the rib cage smiles, the abdomen smiles, the muscles smile and the pelvis smiles...
Maybe we can also refer to a beautiful memory, but I don't want to be too intrusive, 'Oh yes, I remember those beautiful experiences'.

There's a smile in the legs, the knees and in the feet. Maybe draw a little smile on each toenail ☺.

And let the throat smile, the back of the neck smile and the ears smile. Every sound becomes music when the ears smile. The jaws relax, the nose relaxes, the tongue relaxes and the lips relax. Maybe the face can make a really relaxed smile. And maybe to close our session, we can smile at each other; whilst smiling at another person we receive their smile too...

11. How to apply Mindfulness+ in practice?

Well, the good news is that there are many ways to practice mindfulness!

Several practices have been developed and organised in a formal way. Within the framework of Mindfulness Based Stress Reduction (MBSR) by Jon Kabat-Zinn, four main practices can be identified:

1. The body scanner

2. Sitting meditation with different objects of attention:
    - breathing
    - whole body
    - sounds
    - thoughts and emotions
    - open consciousness (renouncing any object of attention)

3. Conscious movements (yoga)

4. Conscious walking

It can be very useful for 'static' practices to create a somewhat 'sacred' place: a place in the house where you feel good. You could possibly set up a small 'altar' area, somewhere to put a candle or other object of attention, equipped with a floor cushion or a comfortable seat.

If possible, also plan your practice at the same time each day, for example, in the morning before diving into daily activities, or in the evening after the end of essential activities.
Paying attentions to these little details and this regularity help to anchor the practice.

It is crucial to find a sitting position in which we are comfortable being still: supported and without strain. To do this it's best is to start from our pelvis: settle it down by placing it comfortably on the cushion or chair with knees at right angles and feet firmly anchored to the ground, preferably without shoes.

We then bring our presence into our pelvis and, from there, let's build our verticality by focusing our attention on our spine from the bottom up: vertebra by vertebra. Place one on top of another, without any discomfort, and follow their natural harmony in the curves of the column.

Once we get to the head we lengthen our cervical vertebrae very slightly and we bring our chin in very slightly; the top of our head is slightly raised as if an invisible thread held us in this natural verticality, with ease.

We then place ourselves in a calm acceptance of the present moment as it is right now, without trying to fill it with anything or change it in any way.

We have already spoken a lot about the body scanner.
We may also choose to practise sitting with an object of attention (such as breathing, sensations in the body, sounds, thoughts or emotions). This is done by by bringing our attention back to that object whenever the mind wanders.

Finally, we can also practise sitting without a specific object of attention by focussing on consciousness itself: on being.

Besides 'static' practices, moving practices are also of great interest.
The best known is undoubtedly yoga which, by combining movement, breathing and concentration, helps us to inhabit the body in full consciousness thanks to gentle stretching, strengthening and balancing exercises. This is a very effective way to learn a lot about yourself, to work with your own limits and to come to feel yourself as a whole (regardless of physical condition or fitness level). It is about adopting attitudes of patience and non-violence towards ourselves.

Ashtanga yoga

In ashtanga yoga, the eightfold path of yoga described in Patanjali's sutras, the method used is based on certain efforts being made. One of these efforts is called 'pratyahara': a way of no longer being distracted by external sensory impressions and directing all your attention inward. 'Pratyahara' means that we will then move our senses away from the outer reality, turning them 180 degrees to look inward.

The next thread of the yoga sutras is called 'dharana': instead of just looking inward, we also make an effort to concentrate. It is the stage of concentrating the mind with the attention fixated on a single point (a point of the body, a candle, an idea, an image, a sound etc). So, you can stare vaguely at something, but you could also look clearly, 'oh I can see the candle, the flashing light and the colour.' There is an element of focus which helps to uncover the deeper layers of self. These deeper layers of self usually take us to a more relaxed place. This is the purpose of the yoga sutras.

The path leads us to complete self-realisation called 'Kayvalya', which means liberation. Patanjali portrays the yogi who has attained kaivalya as an entity who has gained independence from all bondages and achieved the absolute true consciousness. In the yoga tradition this is the ultimate goal. In the Integral Presence philosophy this is half-way to the full realisation of the 21 elements.

Conscious walking

The art of walking meditation involves learning to be mindful while walking, using the movement of walking to cultivate mindfulness and the awakened presence. Different types of attention are utilised from focussing on the components of each step to wide & open attention on the whole body, or on the whole environment.

Finally, beyond the formalised practices in the context of Jon Kabat-Zinn's work, millennia practices have been proven and can certainly inspire you according to your desires of the day.

Meditation on loving kindness

This meditation aims to evoke feelings of kindness, generosity, good will, love and compassion. It then directs these feelings towards oneself and towards others (loved ones, people with whom we have relationships). We can do it for 'neutral' relationships, but also for the people with whom we have a difficult relationship. We can also do it for other living beings and even the life-giving planet itself. This practice helps cultivate strong positive emotions within oneself and can be an antidote to self-criticism. It can also help dispel any feelings of aversion, unwillingness or resentment.

The permanent calm meditation

This meditation directs the mind towards an object (for example a stone or a representation of the Buddha) to allow it to calm down. Alternatively, the attention falls on the shapeless breath. In this way you stay in the 'here and now' without intention. Thoughts may arise, but you don't follow them. Nevertheless, if this does happen, and you slip into the past or the future, you systematically return to the object of focus in a relaxed manner.
The mind is soothed. It becomes like the undisturbed surface of a lake, reflecting everything clearly. Likewise, this practice results in an experience of profound clarity and joy. It also brings more energy and a growing ability to let go of disturbing emotions.

Insight meditation

This practice aims at recognising the nature of our own mind. When distracted, the mind does not have the opportunity to observe itself. In contrast, in the meditative state it becomes possible to look at your own mind: the experiencing one.
One contemplates how thoughts and feelings arise, travel and dissolve in the mind like waves in the sea.
When one reaches the level of direct perception the mind shows its timeless nature, free from any dualistic concept that separates one thing or individual from another.

Once the mind calms down there is a space that emerges quite naturally. In fact it is not a space that emerges; it is a space that is always there: the space of consciousness. This is always there. Our constantly busy mind makes it invisible, but this space is always there. When the mind calms down we create fewer barriers between our perceptions and this space; we can land in this space of lucidity, awareness, clarity and neutrality.

These qualities of consciousness emanate from the Neutral Observer, of whom we have already spoken.

I suggest another little exercise to go to meet him:

Let's do it differently this time: for the next five or ten minutes let's not practise... If we try too hard to contact the Neutral Observer, our full attention will be taken in that trying and we will not be available to simply 'let it come to us'.

So my invitation is more like, 'In the space of freedom that I place myself in here and now, can I receive it if it presents itself?' A useful comparison is that of searching for an elf in the woods. We know that if we make a lot of noise, in actively seeking them out, all the elves run away. It is therefore better to approach things a little differently: to walk quietly, to tune in with nature, to not be too loud, to be gentle, tender and kind... maybe then the elf will show itself...

I like to use this metaphor to illustrate the delicacy involved in discovering the Neutral Observer.
Let's devote five to ten minutes to this 'non-practice' of the effortless search or the effortless discovery of the Neutral Observer.

12. From the meditation cushion to Mindfulness+ in action

Because yes, that is what it is about: how to prolong the benefits of the formal practice of Mindfulness+ into the practical situations of everyday life...?

Regular practice builds a serene detachment from events in us. It is not about indifference and it's not a wall built between us and others, or between us and events; on the contrary, it is a 'fuller' perception of everything that is happening in our life. It is the curious perception of every moment, it is the new discovery, made with our beginner's mind, which I mentioned at the beginning of this book.

Faced with life, with reality, we are indeed always a beginner. In reality the present moment is always new. We have never lived the same moment twice. This awareness allows us to keep our senses completely fresh and open to the creative awareness of each moment. That's why I love this aspect of Integral Presence so much.

It is unlike the mind, which tends to compare perceptions with memories and create a representation of the world: a reality-map of it inside of us. This activity of the mind is obviously essential, but if we are too busy consulting our memory archives, we limit our actual current perception. The time we spend in our memories, comparisons, and mental repertoires takes us away from the true experience of the new, refreshing life that is always pouring forth; this life is full of original manifestations every second.

I have high expectations of the benefits of supra-sensory consciousness, particularly in a world undergoing rapid and uncertain change, provided that the foundations and gradual development of Integral Presence are well established. Otherwise, encounters with the higher dimensions of our Being are a diversion, or an escape, from reality which later results in a painful landing.

In addition to the formal practices mentioned above, a whole range of informal practices can accompany us throughout the day; they are about becoming aware of what is happening in each moment without changing our habits.

For example, let us focus our attention on the sensations in the feet when we walk, on the taste and consistency of our food when we eat, or on the appearance of our environment when we cross it... Let's take a shower consciously by feeling the pleasure of water flowing over the skin, with its warmth and its benefits... Let's observe our usual modes of functioning: our behaviours and reactions...

Cultivate breath awareness in the midst of our activities by paying attention to our breath for a few minutes, several times a day.
When we're behind the wheel, let's take advantage of traffic jams to refocus on our present moment: how does my body react to this forced wait? Are there any tensions that are emerging? Is my heart rate increasing? Are my hands tightening on the wheel? The simple observation and acceptance of what is already there will change our perception of the situation.
Do the same thing in the queue at the supermarket...
Let's take a step back to cultivate loving kindness towards ourselves and others...
These are just a few examples of the many possibilities that exist for developing Mindfulness+.

In conclusion, I would like to share with you an immeasurable benefit discovered from years of practice which is within everyone's reach:

There is no event in life, no matter how painful, that is not modified by a moment of meditative sitting: none!

The worries, the sorrows, the thwarted loves, the despair, the anger and the sadness... if these are accepted, fully felt and deposited in the silence of our awakening consciousness, then they are reduced, refocused more precisely, and will take up less space, becoming manageable.
We know then that they are only transient because nothing is permanent in life and we also discover that we have a lot more strength just to face them; we will not be drowned, we breathe...

Last but not least...

With sincere and repeated practice, supra-sensory consciousness promises us the skills necessary to together shape a human society that spontaneously lives in optimal communion with All That Is. The individual who is unified within himself is also united with humanity and the entire universe.

In essence, Mindfulness+ promotes natural contact with oneself, others and the world.

Further explorations:

- https://janjanssen.bandcamp.com/
- https://the-integral-presence-journey.thinkific.com
- https://www.integral-presence.com/fr/bienvenu-3
- https://www.janjanssen.be/fr/bienvenue-2

Milton Keynes UK
Ingram Content Group UK Ltd.
UKHW021546050124
435486UK00011B/224